Beyond the Players

Referees and Umpires

by Allan Morey

Bullfrog Books

Ideas for Parents and Teachers

Bullfrog Books let children practice reading informational text at the earliest reading levels. Repetition, familiar words, and photo labels support early readers.

Before Reading
- Discuss the cover photo. What does it tell them?
- Look at the picture glossary together. Read and discuss the words.

Read the Book
- "Walk" through the book and look at the photos. Let the child ask questions. Point out the photo labels.
- Read the book to the child, or have him or her read independently.

After Reading
- Prompt the child to think more. Ask: Have you ever seen a referee or umpire at a sporting event? Do you think sports should have them? Why or why not?

Bullfrog Books are published by Jump!
5357 Penn Avenue South
Minneapolis, MN 55419
www.jumplibrary.com

Copyright © 2024 Jump! International copyright reserved in all countries. No part of this book may be reproduced in any form without written permission from the publisher.

Library of Congress Cataloging-in-Publication Data

Names: Morey, Allan, author.
Title: Referees and umpires / Allan Morey.
Description: Minneapolis, MN: Jump!, Inc., [2024]
Series: Beyond the players | Includes index.
Audience: Ages 5–8
Identifiers: LCCN 2023028835 (print)
LCCN 2023028836 (ebook)
ISBN 9798889966500 (hardcover)
ISBN 9798889966517 (paperback)
ISBN 9798889966524 (ebook)
Subjects: LCSH: Sports officials—Juvenile literature. | Sports officiating—Juvenile literature.
Classification: LCC GV735 .M67 2024 (print)
LCC GV735 (ebook)
DDC 796.07/7—dc23/eng/20230726
LC record available at https://lccn.loc.gov/2023028835
LC ebook record available at https://lccn.loc.gov/2023028836

Editor: Jenna Gleisner
Designer: Emma Almgren-Bersie

Photo Credits: NurPhoto SRL/Alamy, cover; Sean Locke Photography/Shutterstock, 1 (left); trekandshoot/Shutterstock, 1 (right); cmannphoto/iStock, 3; Tim Davenport/Alamy, 4, 5, 6–7, 23tl; Mingo Nesmith/Icon Sportswire/AP Images, 8–9; Dan POTOR/Shutterstock, 10–11; Paul Spinelli/AP Images, 12; Aspenphoto/Dreamstime, 13; Mike Stobe/NHLI/Getty, 14–15, 23br; Mikolaj Barbanell/Shutterstock, 16–17, 23tr; Andre Weening/BSR Agency/Getty, 18; Mine Toz/Shutterstock, 19; Lorado/iStock, 20–21; gorodenkoff/iStock, 22tl; fstop123/iStock, 22tr, 23bl; Belish/Shutterstock, 22bl; muzsy/Shutterstock, 22br; GIROMIN STUDIO/Shutterstock, 24.

Printed in the United States of America at Corporate Graphics in North Mankato, Minnesota.

Table of Contents

"Safe!"	4
On the Job	22
Picture Glossary	23
Index	24
To Learn More	24

"Safe!"

We are at a softball game.

Joy slides into home plate.

Is she safe?

Is she out?

The umpire makes the call.

He signals.

"Safe!"

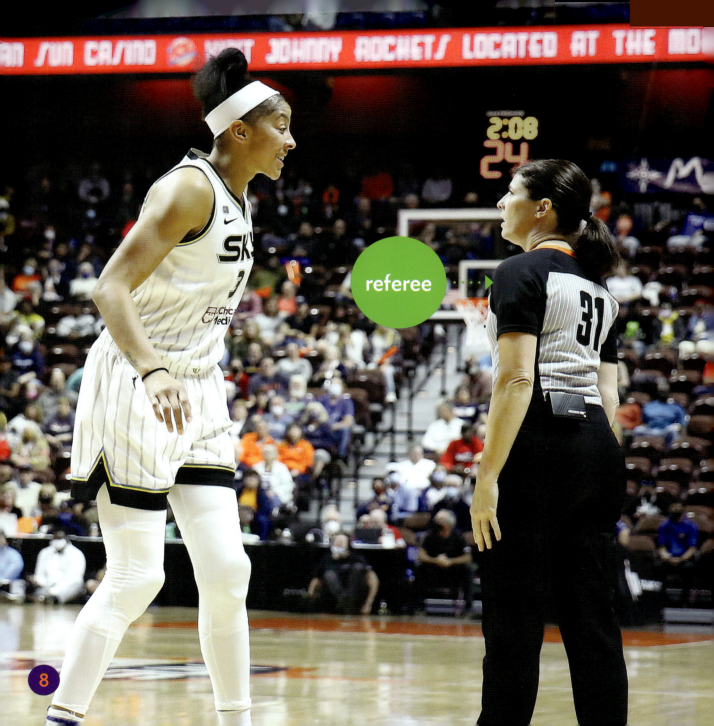

Umpires keep games fair.
So do referees.
They know the rules.

They start the game.
Tom drops the puck!

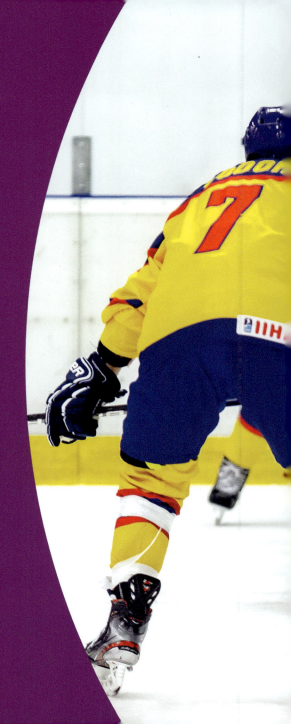

puck

Blake raises his hands. What does it mean?

Touchdown!

A player is hurt.
Timeout!
Jon stops the game.

Amy holds up a card.

It is yellow.

She calls a foul.

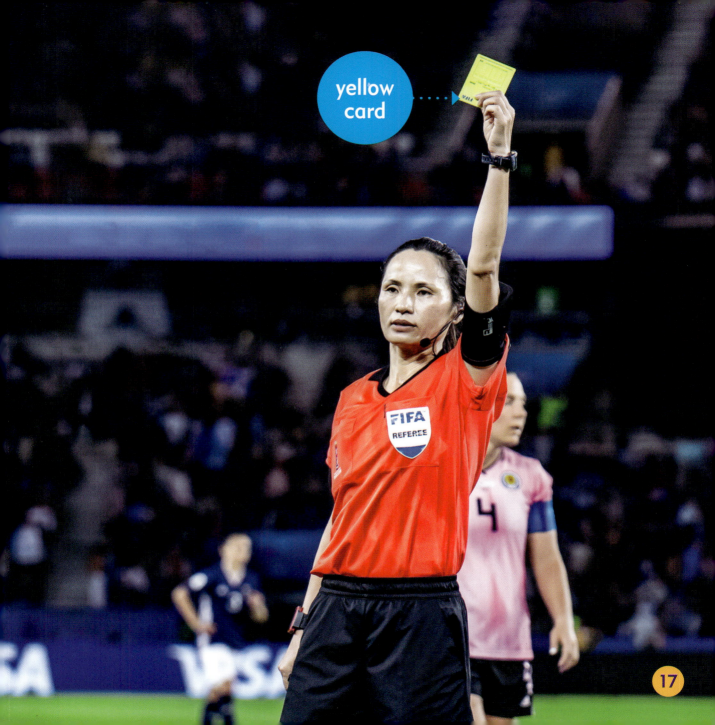

Ed blows his whistle.

The game is over.

Ann raises Tia's arm.
Tia won!

What is your favorite sport?
Do you know its rules?
You could be a referee!

On the Job

Referees and umpires use signals. What do they signal? Take a look!

start and stop of play
They signal when a game or play starts or ends. They also signal timeouts.

score
They signal when there is a score.

winner
They signal who won.

foul
They signal when there is a foul or penalty.

Picture Glossary

call
A decision.

foul
Something done in sports that is against the rules.

signals
Makes a sign or gesture that sends a message.

timeout
A pause in play.

Index

call 6, 16
card 16
fair 9
foul 16
game 4, 9, 10, 15, 18
hands 12
player 15
rules 9, 20
signals 6
timeout 15
whistle 18
won 19

To Learn More

Finding more information is as easy as 1, 2, 3.

❶ Go to www.factsurfer.com
❷ Enter "refereesandumpires" into the search box.
❸ Choose your book to see a list of websites.